La blonde joyeuse et la brune sérieuse. Il a choisi la brune et la blonde s'est suicidée. La brune est morte d'une maladie [illegible] peintres [illegible]oire.

The L[illegible]

BONN[illegible]

Catherine de Duve
in collaboration with the Musée Bonnard

A journey to the South of France, the land of colours

KATE'ART EDITIONS

Le musée Bonnard

IN BONNARD'S DAY

Paris is the place to be, Paris is where everything is happening! The 1889 Universal Exhibition is in full swing and France is celebrating the centenary of the French Revolution.

A tower up into the sky! Gustave Eiffel is building an iron tower 324 metres high on the Champ-de-Mars. Not far away, the painter Paul Gauguin is showing his paintings at the Volpini Café.

The horses' hooves clip clop on the paving stones. Carriages are stopping at the Place de la Concorde. In the Tuileries garden, governesses in wide-brimmed hats are keeping an eye, from a distance, on children playing with hoops or riding donkeys...

In winter, skaters venture onto the ice.

Tourists travel by train and steamship. They photograph each other. What a lovely souvenir of Venice!

Vuillard and Bonnard

BONNARD

Soon the first automobiles are seen on the streets. Clichy Square is full of bustling crowds, shops, restaurants and cafés with outdoor terraces.

Art lovers are introduced to oriental art and the decorative arts by the dealer Samuel Bing.

Ladies take tea in amazing hats bought from milliners' shops.

What should one wear
to the opera?
It's the *Belle Epoque* !

PIERRE

Pierre Bonnard was born on October 3rd, 1867 in Fontenay-aux-Roses, near Paris. His father, Eugène Bonnard, was from the Dauphiné region. He worked at the War Ministry and liked gardens. His mother Élisabeth Mertzdorff was from Alsace. They had three children together, Charles (1864), Pierre (1867) and Andrée (1872). The Bonnards spent their summers in the family country house in Le Grand-Lemps, in Isère, near Grenoble. This is where Pierre, as a child, first discovered nature, flowers and animals.

'I'm going to spend all day doodling pictures'

he wrote before leaving for his holidays in the countryside.

Look how Bonnard paints his garden.

FINE ARTS SCHOOL

At school, Bonnard enjoyed literature, Latin, Greek and philosophy. He also liked drawing. After his baccalaureate, Pierre followed his father's wishes and began to study law in Paris. He also took painting classes at the Académie Julian, where he made friends with Paul Sérusier and Maurice Denis.

Two years later, Bonnard enrolled at the Fine Arts School in Paris. Here he met Édouard Vuillard, who became his great friend. Together they visited galleries and exhibitions, and travelled in Italy and Spain. They discovered the paintings of the impressionist painter Monet*, but also those of Gauguin*, Degas* and Cézanne*. How inspiring!

Bonnard took his box of paints wherever he went: both on holiday, when he had time to paint, and during his military service, when he painted the soldiers.

Like Bonnard, 'doodle' a picture of a garden.

**To find out more, take a look at* The Little Monet, The Little Gauguin, The Little Degas *and* The Little Cézanne *in the same collection.*

NABIS

The young Bonnard was one of the Nabis, a new group of artists founded by Sérusier in 1888. Vuillard, Denis and Vallotton also joined. What did they want to create?

The Nabis used simplified shapes and colours. Some of them were influenced by mystic religious art, others by Japanese art. They saw Gauguin's paintings as a starting point. Like him, they wanted to use intense colours.

Nabis: *the word in Hebrew means 'the initiated' or 'the prophets'. This art movement turned against formal, academic art. They wanted to do something new in the field of graphic and decorative arts.*

Look at these paintings by Bonnard's friends.

Denis
1870 - 1943

Sérusier
1864 - 1927

Vuillard
1868 - 1940

COLOUR

In Paris, all the passers-by seem to be in a great hurry as they scurry along the busy boulevard. Where are they rushing to? It's the universal exhibition!

Look at this picture. Is there any perspective? Do you think the artist painted it quickly?

COLOUR

In Bonnard's work, colour is essential and more important than form.

TECHNIQUE

This picture is made up of juxtaposed colours, applied flatly. The colours seem to be devouring the shapes.

CHAMPAGNE!

His first success! Bonnard designed an advertising poster. He was proud to see it posted up all over Paris and to earn his first 100 francs, and decided to concentrate entirely on his painting. At the age of 22, Bonnard left his job as a lawyer and rented a studio in the Batignolles district.

What a poster! The lady's hair and dress are shown by wavy lines which seem to be running across the picture. The champagne bubbles over joyfully. Everything seems to be dancing against the flat yellow background. Have you noticed how the black lines stand out in this *lithograph*?

Look at the poster. Which brand is it advertising? How many colours can you count? What is the lady holding?

Lithograph: *from litho, stone, and graph, drawing: a design is marked out on a special piece of limestone, which is then used to print a series of pictures.*

REVUE BLANCHE

Bonnard also produced some designs for decorative arts projects: fans, plates and furniture. He also did some drawings for *La Revue Blanche*, a new literary and art review, to which the greatest writers and artists of the time contributed. In particular, he illustrated a book of Paul Verlaine's poetry, commissioned by the famous art dealer Ambroise Vollard.

Apparently, Misia, the wife of the founder of La Revue Blanche, *modelled for this poster*

Compare Bonnard's design with Toulouse-Lautrec's poster.

His friend Toulouse-Lautrec also designed posters

Your turn to think up a poster advertising a brand of champagne.

TUILERIES GARDEN

I'm working on a screen…It shows the Place de la Concorde, with a young mother passing by, with her children, nannies and dogs, and above her, acting as a sort of border, a stopping-place for carriages. All of this is against an off-white background, just like the Place de la Concorde, when it's dusty and looks like a mini Sahara.

This isn't a painting! 'It's the eighth wonder of the world!' declared Bonnard about his screen. The colours were printed one after the other, so that the printed design emerges subtly. Between broad empty spaces, the figures and objects are shown from the smallest to the largest: the frieze of carriages, the railings, the nannies in wide-brimmed hats, the mother and children, the dogs, etc.

Look at the screen. What differences can you see between the carriages? How many children and dogs can you count?

SCREEN

In March 1891, Bonnard showed several pieces of art at the annual exhibition of the Salon des Indépendants, including some decorative panels, *Women in Gardens*.

Find the dog and the cat. Which season do you think each of these panels represents? What format is Bonnard using?

The young Nabi artists were inspired by the elongated shape of *kakemonos* - Japanese pictures rolled around a wooden rod and hung on the wall. These were very decorative.

Like Bonnard, design your own screen.

CROQUET

What a sunny afternoon! The Bonnard family is playing croquet in the shade under the trees. Their patterned clothes look as if they have been cut and pasted onto a lush green background. Figures, in garments like *kimonos*, Japanese clothes, stand out from the background. In the distance, young girls in white dresses are dancing in a circle, laughing.

Who's who? Meet Bonnard's family. Find the artist's signature.

'THE JAPANESE-STYLE NABI'!

Bonnard exhibited this picture at the *Salon des Indépendants* in March 1892. People called him the 'Japanese-style Nabi'!

Salon des Indépendants: *each year from 1884 onwards, the association of independent artists organised an art exhibition in Paris. What was so unusual about it? There was no jury or prize-money, but it enabled artists to show their work to the public.*

Find these details in the picture.

Eugène Bonnard, wearing a straw boater

Andrée Bonnard and her husband, the composer Claude Terrasse

A friend in a printed plaid dress

A circle-dance

A dog and a mallet

A wooden ball and a hoop

MARTHE

Photography

Bronze sculpture

In 1893, when Pierre was 26, he met Maria Boursin, known as Marthe, in Montmartre. She was a little 'wild' and became his model, his muse, his partner and then, in 1925, his wife. He sketched her nude, made sculptures of her, painted her, and photographed her as if he were painting her in a mysterious atmosphere. He seemed to be showing a 'first impression'.

Look at the different techniques used by Bonnard.

Oil painting

Lithograph

Pencil sketch

DAYDREAMING

Jean Terrasse, Pierre Bonnard's nephew, the son of Andrée Bonnard and the composer Claude Terrasse, is sitting at the table. The plates and food have been served but Marthe seems to be elsewhere.... What is she looking at?

Write down what you think Marthe is dreaming about. Find the person hidden behind Marthe, with the soup tureen.

MA ROULOTTE

From 1900 onwards, Bonnard spent a part of every year in the country. He aspired to the 'country life'. In 1912, he bought a little house beside the Seine, at Veronnet in Normandy. He called it 'Ma Roulotte' ('The Caravan'). Five kilometres away, in Giverny, lived the elderly impressionist painter Claude Monet. They paid each other neighbourly visits.

In Normandy, Bonnard tried to develop a new, more personal, style of art. He was constantly drawing, seeking and beginning to paint landscapes.

I wanted to forget everything I knew, I'm trying to learn new things. I'm constantly drawing. And after drawing comes the composition, which must be balanced. If the composition of a picture is good, half the work is already done The art of composition is so important, that using just black and white, pencil, pen, and an engraver's chisel, you can achieve results which are as complete, and as beautiful, almost, as if you were using the whole range of colours...

Here is Ma Roulotte, drawn in pen and ink. Look closely at Bonnard's drawing technique. He has used different brushstrokes for different parts of the drawing. Imagine a story about this house...

Pierre and Marthe beside the Seine

CÔTE D'AZUR

It was just like something from the Arabian Nights. The sea, the yellow walls, the reflections as full of colour as the light itself.

Bonnard discovered the South of France. He loved and was inspired by everything! He stayed in Saint-Tropez. He often went back there. He visited other places on the Côte d'Azur: Marseille, Toulon, Grasse, Antibes, Cannes... He met other artists there, who had also been attracted by the Southern sun: Matisse*, Renoir*, Manguin, Signac, Maillol…

Bonnard was bowled over by the nature and light of the South of France. He found everything inspiring! The exuberant plant-life, the hills, the sea, the warm wind... He wanted to paint all of this in his own special style. Nature exploded into sparkling masses of colour. What a paradise!

Look how the artist uses his colours.

**To find out more, take a look at* The Little Matisse *and* The Little Renoir *in the same collection.*

LANDSCAPES

'A direct view over nature... the best thing that can happen to a painter'
Letter from Pierre Bonnard to Henri Matisse, 1940

Plunge into the scenery at Le Cannet. Which of these pictures do you prefer?

TUB

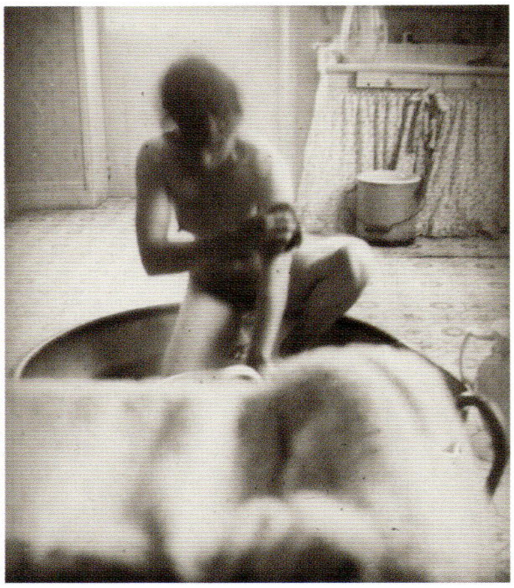

At the time, people often washed in large round tubs filled with water

Bonnard took photographs as if he were painting a picture, with sensitivity. Marthe loved having a bath. She needed her baths.

Bonnard also made many sketches, which he used as a basis for his paintings. Before him, another artist, Edgar Degas*, had painted women washing.

This is one of Bonnard's sketches. Compare it to the pastel drawing by Degas.

To find out more, take a look at The Little Degas *in the same collection.*

BATH

Bonnard uses brushstrokes to make the reflections gleam on the wall-tiles, the chequered floor, the enamel bath, the water and Marthe's skin... Everything is dancing in the light! It's like a mosaic of coloured sequins, shimmering and creating a fairytale atmosphere. Such is the artist's magic touch!

The outlines are vague and shifting. Doesn't it look like golden rain? The bath tub could be a pearly shell, and Marthe could be the Goddess Venus.

How does Bonnard play with the effects of the light? Where is the light coming from?

LE BOSQUET

Bonnard became a well-known artist. Duncan Phillips, the American art collector, bought some of his artworks. Two years later, Bonnard travelled to Pittsburgh in the United States, where he was on a jury, and soon the French painter was exhibiting in New York. He was now internationally famous!

At the age of 59, Bonnard bought Le Bosquet, a little pink house in Le Cannet, high up in the hills above Cannes, 'the last street of the high country'. The house had a wonderful sweeping view over the Mediterranean and the blue mountains. The artist made some changes to it, and added a balcony, a modern bathroom for Marthe, and a studio.

Here, he was right in the heart of nature. For more than 22 years, Bonnard painted his house and its surroundings. Tirelessly, over and over again, he painted the almond tree, the olive trees and the date palm in his garden.

Bonnard liked walking. Here is the countryside around his house. Look how he uses pastels.

PANORAMA

The leaves of the palm trees open up to reveal the stage of a natural theatre. The red tiles of the houses and the tops of the yellow plane trees add definition to the landscape, which gradually merges into the Estérel mountains. The blues and the greens become almost grey.

Is there perspective in this picture? We see objects at different distances, which provides depth. Bonnard spoke of pictures 'vibrating with life'. Could this be the influence of the Provençal painter Paul Cézanne*?

Look at this large painting. Where was the painter when he painted this landscape?

To find out more, take a look at The Little Cézanne *in the same collection.*

FRUITS

Everything is calm in the house... Life goes on peacefully. Time seems to have stopped. In the dining room, Marthe, leaning on the table, is playing with a cat. Can you see it?

The room is bathed in golden light. The walls are painted in warm colours, a mixture of Naples yellow and vermilion, so that the room reminds us of a sweet orange.

Find the fruit bowl in the picture, based on this sketch. What colour is the cat?

CAT

Bonnard liked animals. He drew them and photographed them with his nephews and nieces. They were part of family life.

What a round cat! Like Japanese artists, Bonnard simplified the cat's shape in a humorous way. The cat's body seems to have become a decorative object.

What object does the cat's shape remind you of? Think of it and draw it in the space below.

COMPOSITION

Marthe has poured water from the white kettle, on the checked tablecloth, into the tea pot. Through the window we can make out dusk falling. The composition is sketched out in pencil, then coloured with watercolours. Bonnard's pictures and drawings are like the artist himself: simple and unassuming.

Where are we? Find the radiator, the kettle and the teapot.

Bonnard

STUDIO

In his studio, Bonnard didn't stretch his canvasses over a frame or use an easel. He preferred to buy rolls of canvas and cut it to the size he wanted. He then tacked several white canvasses up on the wall using drawing pins. Why not paint several pictures at once? One on the mezzanine, and, below, another in front of the window.

On the mezzanine, we can make out certain objects.

Bonnard on the mezzanine in his studio

Find a table made of woven bamboo, the railing, a basket, an oil lamp, a high stool and the window.

MIMOSA

What can the painter see from his studio window?
Find the rail and the hidden figure.

'BONNARDING!'

Bonnard was now famous. But he couldn't stop himself adding final touches to his canvasses! Often, he would make alterations to his pictures, right in front of the museum attendants. 'Pierre is bonnarding again!', laughed his friends. The Bonnards finally settled in Le Cannet. Bonnard's friends came to visit: the painters Henri Matisse, Auguste Renoir and the Swiss collector Hahnloser.

Bonnard and the Hahnlosers in front of the almond tree

Soon afterwards, the Second World War broke out. The Bonnards stayed in Le Cannet. Pierre walked, and drew his garden and the surrounding area in his diary.

On the day when Marthe died in 1942, Pierre stayed by himself and just drew a small cross in his diary. Finally, spring arrived. The mimosas and sweet-smelling blossom of the almond tree in the garden were coming into flower. The almond tree was the subject of his final picture.

Bonnard in Matisse's studio in Nice, around 1929

Bonnard died in Le Cannet on January 23rd, 1947 at the age of 81. 'He who sings is not always happy'.

Texts and illustrations: Catherine de Duve
Concept and creation: Kate'Art Editions
Proofreading: Véronique Serrano, Chief curator at the Musée Bonnard, Carole Lenglet and the Public service department of the Musée Bonnard

PHOTO CREDITS
Works by Pierre Bonnard: BESANÇON: Musée des Beaux-Arts et d'Archéologie: *Place Clichy*, 1912: p.3. – **LE CANNET: Musée Bonnard: Photos Jean-Michel Drouet:** *Self-portrait against the Light*, 1923: p.1 – *Garden in Le Cannet*, 1945: p.4 – *Luncheon, Marthe Bonnard and Jean Terrasse*, 1916: p.15 – **Photos Frédéric Aubert:** *The Skaters*, 1897: p.2 – *Figures in the street*, 1889: p.7 – *The Dining Room*, 1930: p.24 – *Cup of tea by the radiator*, 1932: p.26 – *Dining Room in Arcachon*, 1931 : p.27 – **Photos Yves Inchiermann:** *Nannies' Promenade - frieze of carriages (detail from the screen)*, 1891: p. 2, p.10 - *Portrait of a woman in a straw hat*, 1903: p.3 –*Self-portrait*, 1904: p.4 –*Poster for France Champagne E. Debray*, 1891: p. 8 – *Poster for la Revue blanche*, 1891: p. 9 –*Nude in Profile*, 1917: p.14 – *Nude (lithography)*, 1930: Cover, p.14– *Nude no.194*, 1919-1920: p.14 – *Naked young girl standing*, 1906: p.14 – *Ma Roulotte*, 1915: p.17 – *Landscape, sunset*, 1926: p.18 – *Landscape at Le Cannet*, 1923-1926: p.19 – *Landscape at night, Cap d'Antibes*, 1912: p. 19 – *Nude*, 1920: p. 20 – *The House in the hills*, 1943: p.22 – *Fruit basket*, 1930: p.24 –*The Cat*, 1920: p.25 – *The Studio at Le Bosquet*, 1935: p.28. – *Almond tree*, 1930: p.30 – **NEW YORK: MET** – *The Bathroom*, 1932: p.21 – **PARIS: Musée d'Orsay:** *The Box*, 1908: p.3 – **Photo Dist. RMN/Patrice Schmidt:** *Twilight also called The Game of Croquet*, 1892: p.12-13 (details) – *View of Le Cannet*, 1927: p.23 – *Dining room in Le Cannet (pencil on paper)*, 1930: p.24 – *Dining room at Le Cannet (oil on canvas)*, 1932: p.24. – **Musée d'Art Moderne:** *Nude in the bath*, 1936: p.21 – **Collection Centre Pompidou: Photo Dist. RMN/Philippe Migeat:** *Studio with Mimosa*, 1939: p.29 – **VERNON: Musée de Vernon:** *Sun at Vernon*, 1915: p.16 – **ZÜRICH: Kunsthaus:** *Decorative panels - Women in the garden*, 1890-1891: p.11 – **Private collection:** *Place Clichy*, 1906-1907: p.3

Works by other artists: Toulouse-Lautrec: Le Cannet: Musée Bonnard: photo 360médias/ Yann Coatsaliou: *Poster for the Revue blanche*, 1895: p.9 – *Landscape of Cannet, (watercolor, gouache and pencil)*, no date: p.19 – **Denis: Saint-Germain-en-Laye: Musée Départemental Maurice Denis:** *Madame Ranson with cat*, 1892: p.6 – **Sérusier: Paris: Musée d'Orsay:** *The Talisman*, 1888: p.6 – **Vuillard: Brussels: MRBAB:** *The Two schoolboys*, 1894: p.6 – **Degas: Paris: Musée d'Orsay:** *The Tub*, 1886: p.20.

Photographs: LE CANNET: Musée Bonnard: Photo Patrice Schmidt: *Roussel with Vuillard photographing Bonnard (Venice)*, 1899: p.2 – *Marthe in the tub*, 1907: p.20 – *A cat jumps onto Andrée Terrasse's dress (Noisy-le-Grand)*,1898: p.25 – **Photos George Auclaire:** *Marthe sitting on the bed, seen from the back*, 1899-1900: p.14 – *Bonnard, Marthe and the Hahnlosers, circa 1927*: p.22 – *Bonnard in his studio at Le Bosquet*: p.28 – **Anonymous:** *Bonnard and the Hahnlosers in front of the almond tree at Le Bosquet*: p.31– **Anonymous:** *Bonnard as an odalisque in Matisse's studio in Nice*, circa 1929: p.31 – **Indivision A.A. Ostier:** *Portrait of Pierre Bonnard, Le Cannet*, 1941: p.31 – **Archive:** *Poster for the 1889 Universal Exhibition*: p.2

Acknowledgements: Véronique Serrano, Chief curator of the Musée Bonnard, Carole Lenglet, Public service department of the Musée Bonnard, the Bonnard Estate, Eric Vaes, Gabriela Nicole Gonzalez, Ophélie Legast, Martina Cappuccio, Julie Verschueren, Sandra Mangoubi, Véronique Lux and all those who helped to create this book.

Visit our online shop: www.kateart.com